ARRHYTHMIA

ALSO BY EMILY VAN KLEY

The Cold and the Rust

ARRHYTHMIA

EMILY VAN KLEY

POEMS

 A KAREN & MICHAEL BRAZILLER BOOK
PERSEA BOOKS / NEW YORK

Persea Books, Inc.
90 Broad Street
New York, NY 10004

Library of Congress Cataloging-in-Publication Data

Names: Van Kley, Emily, author.
Title: Arrhythmia : poems / Emily Van Kley.
Description: First edition. | New York : Persea Books, [2021] | "A Karen &
    Michael Braziller book." | Summary: "A tribute to queer friendship, these
    poems weave chronic grief (a damaged planet, social injustice) with the stab
    of a loved one's sudden absence-of what happens to the vibrant particulars of
    a life when it ends"—Provided by publisher.
Identifiers: LCCN 2021039892 | ISBN 9780892555390 (trade paperback)
Subjects: LCGFT: Poetry.
Classification: LCC PS3622.A5854939 A88 2021 | DDC 811/.6—dc23
LC record available at https://lccn.loc.gov/2021039892

Book design and composition by Rita Lascaro
Manufactured in the United States of America.

For Michael Henson (1982–2012)
who shimmers—and shimmies—on

CONTENTS

ONE

DEAR SKULL

beloved braincase, body's bleeding heart
helmet law

dear ribs thick with implied meat, disused central
railroad, reverse spec house unplumbed
to propitious frame

dear double-strung forearm, dear violin bow,

dear pachyderm-eared pelvis,

dear barnacle spine—

tolerate this animate interlude, nervous tic of cell & swoosh,
elasticity & vein

& you'll emerge, democratically beautiful,

armature to nothing

you'll make the case for stasis, grow
each year more ravishingly still

yes, the flesh is weak,
but you are forged of patience,

ill inclined to cheer or mourn
the extraneous

—respiration, cartilage—as it trundles away

INTRODUCTION

Now there is no rush.
Weeks pass. When it appears—
the pine-etched marker

your husband has selected
& will someday share—
I visit as if a person,

become acquainted,
trace the slab with its flat-
faced mountain & whorl

of forest, its linked
rings. Afterwards wander
in that dazed parenthetical

state that comes upon
me now, slides in
irresolute between

word & deed—intention
upended, understanding
stammered. Some rows

west, a heart-shaped stone
bears another pair
of mens' names, another

set of birth years, one
unhinged to the future,
the other awful

in its symmetry,
lifespans similarly askew.
Nothing left to know or

misbelieve, I imagine
a welcoming, a watching
over. I touch the caduceus

beside the name of the one
still living & hope some
afternoon I'll happen

upon him, the good doctor.
I'd take his hand, show him
your serene square;

together we'd correlate
disaster. Yet the truth,
confounding, unsearchable:

the introduction I most
want to make is
of the dead to the dead.

DUSK

It's not so much
that light leaves

as that dark affixes.
First the bunched green

needles of the Ponderosa
beyond my window

hashmark flat
black. Next,

the neighbors' red
door oxbloods,

thickens to the color
of absence,

fingery rhododendrons
stationed like cut-out

sentries at either side.
Dark darts

through the sky's
grey glut of clouds,

pulled to every
tree & plant

& made thing
like powdered

iron to a magnetic
pole. & only when shadow

owns all that has shape
below the heavens

does it seep back
to blue the air

that shade of deep
ocean just before

creatures give up
on eyes. Dark doesn't

fall. It completes.
A mercy, considering

how full-spectrum
the day you folded

like a dropped towel
while stepping

out of the shower.
How artless the sun

through the bathroom
window as your husband

caught a cab home
from work—

& so we arrive,

as every poem
does lately—

to find he couldn't
hold you—

each poem begins
believing there's something

to be said about
night, or the trees—

SURFACE

Start particulate; press
to something implacable.

Dust, welcome to your future
as stone. Stone, meet

wind & water, oracles
of your destiny as dust.

What starts as surface
braids below, is uncovered
later: more surface.

Place your particular soles
upon any exposed dirt. Imagine
roots twisting like hairs

through ligament & callus,
parting cells to pass
from body to stratum

& down. Grit into it,
the boulders you'd pass,

the earthworms lolling.
Pulverized leaves, leathered
insect eggs, rusted eye-bolts:

all manner
of the dead & discarded,

a process for everything
with few exceptions,

certainly not you
standing above as if apart
for now

BODIES

Try as we might, we can't
help believing heaven is up,
though the truth is we've

no purchase in this black ice
universe, our language
skidding from one nothing

to another—direction, shape.
The what of it: selfless,
unthinged. Also lacking

edges, though scientists
say it's a tattered
dress, always flaring

outward, if there were out,
in. We stand on the front
porch when spring comes,

our feet bare, scarves
solved cosines mapped
to hooks on the mudroom

wall. We tilt our necks,
believing we look heavenward,
while in fact we're turning

pirouettes in mad
overlap—orbit, daybreak,
galactic year—plus

plunging headlong
into a nothing so thick
it feeds itself with light

but never shines. Closest,
perhaps, at night, dark-
drunk, when we click

the lamp switch and hope
there is no one we don't
know standing

in the doorway, and we
come to understand,
while we wait

for our pupils to sharpen,
that whatever called us
stayed behind in the bafflement

we woke from and we are
alone—if safe, not certain.

GROUNDSKEEPING

One week after your funeral,
someone has laid back the sod
squares cut to let your pine

box pass. The grass
sun-frazzled, the dirt overlapped
& gapping—it's been the driest

September following the driest
August since before you
were born. Tidy friend,

this mess you have no
means to redress—
why does it break me?

Let's pretend our doom
is still mostly individual.
Let's say the rains are likely

to return, stitch a fine
green over you, erase
these clumsy seams

which call to mind the chest
unzipped below, the coroner's
tools hounding perfect

tulip-bulb organs gone
inexplicably senseless to the flash
seasons of breath & blood.

Dear, today I leave you
a rose, some aster,
which next week I'll return

to clear, wilted & brown. Autumn
collects such lesser deaths
until its scale tips to winter.

My own cells spill & gather
for time as yet unmeasured,
while water pends

until it can't help falling,
& the fields brighten, bleak
with vigor under a sky silked grey.

HOUSEBOAT

Or to live on the water
in saltbox cedar shake.
Rain, the windows weeping,
the ocean drinking itself

to a stagger, sipping ice
from splintered poles.

Grief swells like damp
doorjambs but the stove

and sink are too petite,
the stairs too miniature,
everything in place

and cleverly fastened,
which means our sadness
should arrive in sensible
measure, even if we exist

in the rumble of doom's
double drumbeat, even if
our models for survival

scatter like facecards in a stiff
wind. Watch us set aside

money in hopes to someday
stop working. When April

warms early, see us
seed tomatoes in terra
cotta, leave off weeding

and coax our skins to echo
chamber—close a thousand
tiny distances until we multiply,

unchart. Love, we are not
brave. We are bodies. Saline,
among other suspensions.
Insipid season:

our intentions fallow.
Our heat bill halves.

Behind the spillway, the lake's
been closed on account
of snails' pathologic
flourish. Starboard,

the paper-thin bustle
of night moths
frilling northward

while salmon slant rhyme
the mouths of rivers
they've known since birth.

CHASTENED

*The mind is the result of the functioning
of our billions of neurons and the soul
a misunderstanding.*
                    —Dick Swaab

A word is so brittle,
confection

of the mind's
pretty.

My grandfather calls,
his accented English

nestled egg-safe
in a nowhere

of precisely timed pulses.
You had a birthday,

femke, *I didn't forget.*

* * *

To say requires such
certainty. I would like

your opinion. I reserve
the right, etc. Hours I chase

a flicker along the edge
of my thoughts' reel

and nothing. I want to tell
the tendency of light

through the season's first
snow but can't grasp

observation's
antecedent, sound

for what I see.

* * *

A nod in the river
asserts

a stone
anchored below.

* * *

Decades
my grandfather

drove delivery in south
Chicago, counted seconds

between stoplights,
cursed seldom

and in a tongue
I never learned.

Sitting shotgun,
I loved

each intersection
for how he'd point, *Now,*

turn the light green.

* * *

Some thoughts are so self–
impressed as to suggest

that thoughts make a net,
a meaning. Others admit

they're no more
than trinkets, exercises

in obsolescence, hiccoughery.
Lacked words

haunt the language
where they might

be thought.

* * *

How unscientific: this attempt
to cut each said thing

down to its mettle.
Trifling, as if order

were to be made
beyond each entanglement

of genome, nerve.

INTRODUCTION

At least once each day I learn
you've died. Not the result
of forgetting. Now

the fault of the spring forsythia
so spectacularly out of hiding,
now of the tax form's ornate

instructions, now the baying
cat intent on breakfast—
anything to fill the mind

before it empties again, exposes
the fact of your absence like sand
that underscores the tide,

like a terrible agate toothing
from the center of a moment plain
as stone. Perhaps some truths,

too vast to be grasped, must
instead accrue—ice over
winter water. So cue

this glitterati of grief
on a plane over Minneapolis,
city lights like thrown

coins, mighty Mississippi cracked
black down the center, all water
the same whatever its millennial

digressions, whatever its sojourn
through culvert or kidney
or cloud. Let's say the problem

is one of momentum. Your life
by most measures less than half-
lived. Decades phantom

limb the date dash date
which means to stand
as your full sum. What then

of your hungers, wakened
that September morning
as every other?

What of the vitality
which rose from you like heat
from asphalt, more

than one body could use?
If your acts, once begun,
reach completion, hello,

hello, are you still with us?
If the planted bulbs
bloom, if the referendum

passes, if your husband,
reading saved journals,
finds himself newly loved?

RELATIVITY

I stood inside the tree
which had survived burning.

Its sapwood was a soft lip
below the bark. Its heartwood

had been kept dead
as a porch column at the
center,

so when the fire
came there would be

something to sacrifice.
Flames entered, smothered,

left a periphery
impertinent with life.

* * *

Below any grove, a sunk
thicket of clasp and microbe.

Site of negotiations.
Shared root cellar stocked

with sunlight's drunk-down
syrup, fungus-mined

minerals threaded
from thorax, litter, stone.

Elsewhere the mantis
hatches 1,000 young,

snacks on the proximate
and birth-stunned.

Procreation: so nutritious.
Life: it takes and it gives.

Each night a velvet painting
of curtains closing

and no one ever
becomes the curtain.

The frangipani for a moment
overrun with tiny

exaggerated elbows,
ambulant spores that disperse

in all the ways
nature intends.

EN SITIO

I.
Not bi but quasi-coastal.
Five minutes from our front door
the ocean ravels.

Tides fill & skelter.
Gulls fuss over errant
mussels, drop oyster shells

for cars to crush. Beside the building
where my love works, creosote-
laced mud rises for hours each day,

grit in the bowl of a drained
washbasin. I stay home, am
whelmed, inch by laggard inch.

Outside, the milky air means
rain approaching, across town
& forever moving east,

having traced the Pacific's
latitudinal largesse, now
in a fervor of significance

dampening its first
leaves & stone since landfall
at a Russian island, lately Japanese.

II.
Question: parsed pendulum,
brace & milestone.

Answer: long enough to be
practiced, if yet unsure.

III.
We live below the exchange.
Our shorelines stuttered,
tectonic, islands strewn

like snapped necklaces,
our salmon mercurial, & not
in the interesting emotional way.

IV.
Question: lumberjack verve,
a plea for concurrence.

Answer: stasis—desire to precipice
the head of a pin marking you are here.

NONSOMNOLENT

We wake ardent, we wake
concave, open our eyes
in a snit of singularity.

We wake wily
at the business end
of ongoing diminishment.

We wake after dreams
so arch, so full of twee
villainy, it's no wonder

we're always getting up
to leave. Nightgowns
are errant around legs

and torsos, so we wake
without them. We wake
sweat saronged, latticeless.

We wake to a breast
garden—pretty much
what everyone has always

suspected. Our sleep
pends, diasporic. We sleep
unctuously in summer.

Our love is official
now. We are an institution
unto each other. When

she ships her legs
to the mattress's farthest
admonition, it is breath

breaking. We wake
in brazen arrangements.
You wonder

so I'll tell you: we are
incredible in bed.

IN THE EVENT ALL INSTRUCTIONS
HAVE BEEN LOST (SOLSTICE)

To create, one must tend
a small plot of melancholy.

To love, freely forfeit
what she can least afford to lose.

Darkest night, what do you offer
in the way of counsel

to we who wrap each new
disaster close as a dressing

gown & step out, sightless,
into coming hours like groves

of trees planted we know not
when or by whom?

If we hold each other, one hand
stays pressed to skin forever,

while the other is already
peeling garlic to be fed

to dinner's soup. Even this day—
the year's most foreshortened—

has in fact only traveled
south to lounge at the horizon.

It's true the moon's just smoke
and mirrors, a giant trick

of reflection. But praise
it anyway—our own brightness

equally borrowed, faces cloaked
in the age-old glow of a ruckus

gone on long enough
to raise the dust of us.

DÉNOUEMENT

Not on purpose you kept
your death for yourself, stepped

from the shower unaware
bade blood could forget
to answer. Arrhythmia.

Crimeless victim. Your ♥
stopped because your heart

stopped. Hidden until the deed
had spelled itself into hours. Until
you'd missed work, worried

people insufficiently to match
the undoing they encountered,

the few still-damp curls to say
that in the morning the body
had been sitting down to its usual

feast of intention. The wrong
not so much committed as wrought.

* * *

Two years since your younger brother
took the first turn—broken
ankle, blood clot. Then, your parents

bought four gravesites, looking
to the far future, they thought.

Of course they neglected
your husband, the vows, the silk
ties, the house amongst ivy—

at that time assuming a lesser
severity of love between men,
believing it a weakness

you'd relinquish when the flesh
no longer held sway. They've since

relented, a marvel I wish you hadn't
had to lose your sight to see.

* * *

Now, your mother's illness:
nothing particularly
nameable. Auto-immune.

Your friends, poor substitute
for sons at her bedside,
keep watch in the white room.

We say she's dying of grief—
diagnosis for a novel of manners—
but the work is athletic,

impolite. Her face lit
with effort, breath Herculean,

machinery jeering
as her knees jab, her arms
and legs puppet, unfavored

toy in a toddler's
tantrumed hands.
All this for no final flush

of victory—only the scripts
we scribble and stuff
in each other's pockets: he and he

left without lingering,
she lingered, then left.

SPAN

Earth tilts & winter night
spills its threshold.
4 pm: the Greyhound's

cabin dusks. Passengers
ball coats & miniature
pillows against windows,

let their eyes stray shut.
We are, most of us,
diurnal. Across the aisle

a woman summons
her overhead lamp.
She knits spotlit,

her needles orchestral;
yarn climbs the ladder
of her lap & legs. Her red

wool shirt & hair
trimmed close are proof
I could love her, if time

ran a different slant, if
I had boarded this bus
undeared & on fire.

Later, at the reading,
a new poet claims a heart
in possession of all

its chambers cannot
be crushed. She hasn't yet
learned: pinhole what's vital

& no kind of strength
will scaffold. I want
a heart to be so butch

& beautiful, pounding beers
in a dive bar, waiting
for exactly me. But a heart

is a switchboard,
indebted to wayward
electricities. Lines

cross. Outages occur.
The morning M lost
his flawless sense

of rhythm, Earth
was poling through a night
that extends beyond

the known & imagined.
This same night.
How absurd I am

to fear it, to believe
the day lengthens,
or that the dark relents.

MEMORIAL

Planted after my grandparents'
war, the oaks
fend Legion Avenue,

seven decades undesecrated
by saw or pruning shear.

Trees don't mean
to mean anything, but death

demands a symbol, doesn't
it?—having no color
or outline of its own.

Root-heavy, they conform
to character, coerce
sidewalks to salute the sky.

* * *

In high school, men
in butter-colored uniforms

summoned me from class.
Their dead were old, unlike

the dead of current wars.
I rode in their vans
to the cemetery,

unpacked my battered
coronet.

They presented
flags, their half-turns
precise, arthritic.

I was grown enough to want
to sound mournful,

my aperture brittle
in fall winter spring cold.

One key to press,
one note to follow,
no one being called.

* * *

In winter the oaks make
a great show of sturdiness,
holding up armfuls of snow.

But one January the sky
flubs protocol, sends down

ice thick as ermine to snap
branches at their crosshairs,

the road such a giant's
briar it's a week before
the bus can pass.

Workers cinch trunks
with spraypaint
so that, come spring,

the city knows to send
climbers in matching
vests who will stump

the trees, one by one,
crown to ground.

TWO

THE SPRINGS

We drank the water, though it stank
        of sulfur & ran in rivers white

with algae like preachers' beards.
        We uncrossed our ankles,

loosened our stays. The men
        didn't notice. Our faces

pearled. Fog drifted.
        Our bones became

visible; they were feathers
        under our skin. We laughed,

our breath smelling of old eggs,
        already knowing we'd live

through two wars, would survive
        turning into mothers,

& lose the men.
        When the resort-keeper

came with his camera
        we kept still

one full second. Kept
        still, but we were brimming.

We were lighthouses.
        We ruined his film.

EROTICA

When she asked to move in I didn't
Stipulate marriage, because not our struggle,
And anyway who wants to be an owned
Thing, a wife? But I was not without rules,
And the rules sprouted vows, and soon
Another woman stood before us,
Saying there must be something to bless,
Some rings. In effect, married. Now
We wade toward middle age, its eddies.
We lawn mow. We pass on the gayby,
Though certain cells weighed in on that one,
Too. We watch people die, and know we have
No end game. Another two years, we say.
Until the car stops running. Until
The kiwi vine blooms. In the quiet
House we wash and rinse the same
Two glasses. We put out poison for rats
In the chickenyard and hope the chickens
Won't eat poisoned rats. We drive
Through wildfires, are forced to relinquish
Travel plans. Have we learned Applicable
Skills? Do we have Something to Contribute?
Tonight it's black holes again, caught
Breath. The body, arms overhead, feet
Stretching beyond what the eye can
See. We wake to the aspirant councilwoman's
Partisans cramming photos of the presumed
Homeless in our screen door, saying
Downtown we shouldn't have to feel
Embarrassed or unsafe. Galled, we chop
Alder beneath spiders hung like bunting

In the carport. Motion-sensed, fluorescent.
With a maul it's not the blade that matters,
But the necessary weight, the right distance to fall.

EQUITY

Bohème lace-front tulips in the yard,
and the fact that there is a yard
with its culled abundance—
green, green, slapdash dandelion,
upturned petticoats of crabgrass,

lien everywhere, though money
is imaginary, never more
than when you promise to pay
half the rest of your life in numbers
you hope will go on ticking

across a screen. Where I live
we still have water, so much
it won't balance on the clouds'
high shelves, crashes over
our heads all fall all spring

and winter, folds us at the stem
so we die more often just
before the sun comes due.
At the title company, we sign
inch-thick contracts no one

understands, and if we're pale
as paper it's likely we'll find out
later the terms were good. The green
is not in on this, the forsythia
breaks forth uncalculating,

a monstrosity of yellow, generous
to all in equal measure, or perhaps
only to itself, some visiting
wings. The hawthorne's
swallowed rings trace a century

of sundowns, though the auditor's
map has purged its red tell. Money:
so imaginary it's deathless,
so real it static-clings
each mistaken generation.

Officially, the yard is a parcel.
The hawthorne belongs
to my neighbor.
The maple is mine.

ELECTROMAGNETIC

The small-town science teacher's
sternest warnings

concerned the murderous
capacity of lightning. Arms
stabbing like irked

storks, he'd demonstrate
bolts pounding telephone

lines, striking
from water taps.
He'd swoon from desk

to desk—the path
of rapt spheres transgressing

walls and windows—
luminous, apparitional,
capable in one

cat-like brush of killing
you cold.

Later the girl woke
to every thunderstorm,
limbs staticked,

always in the flash calm
before a knowing globe of light

would crest
her bedroom eaves,
glide on secret

physics through addled
air to freeze-tag

her and her sister
in their metal bunks, then gleam
away to extinguish

the rest
of the whisperless house.

* * *

Harmless by comparison:
vertical branches drawn down
on summer afternoons

to even the charge between
earth and sky—unless

you're the man hit
seven times,
who begins to believe

storm clouds capable
of pursuit. Who keeps

a pan of water
in his truck, precaution
against recurrent

bouts of bursting
into flame. He isn't

wrong. It keeps happening.
Which begs
the question of volition.

How we prefer
"unlucky" to "cursed."

* * *

In the concert hall's Faraday cage
your band played compositions
for stars falling, presented

an award in your name.
Friend, your face

beamed overhead,
a mechanism of widening
light. In the front row

your mother ailed, oxygen
tubes rasping—she'd aged

twenty years in the three
since you and your brother
broke frequency. Your father

applauded, his smile
perpetually fortified for alarm.
When the last note fled

he helped his wife
to her feet. Past their bedtime,
he said, and took his leave.

INTRODUCTION

At first I thought
I'd become
a friend of death,

your body-less
body double,
reassuring, contractual,

doing its duty.
Fantastical reservoir
of each gone

beloved, their excess
intelligence, their surplus
affection and pain.

Place-holder
made portal, anti-
address to which our love

letters might still
be addressed.
I thought death

was in it with me,
holding you a hair's
breath on the other side

of matter's silk screen.
All our lives
we play at certainty.

Today I think death's
no more than crass
erasure, word

affording undue
substance, name
for that which merits

none. My own time
left feinting into a vast
lack. Flash in the pan.

To speak of death
as nothingness,
a silence—

gross overstatement.
To say "death."
To say anything at all.

EFFLUVIUM

Often we bled
afterwards.
A seep high
in the nostrils,
then red. Or
our heads pounded
& we slept
for hours in dark
rooms, waited
for our thoughts
to unbrick.

Our sight bent. Our
ears would warm
as if wasp-stung.
It wasn't worth it,
but we'd forget.
The lake a colossus,
backhanding Canada,
drilling itself deeper
than any mine. So
cold even in shallows
our legs would lock;
we'd break our
breath getting
back to shore.

Better to park beside
the chemical plant's
outlet, swim where
water—siphoned
somewhere unseen—

returned warm
from its dizzied,
latch-hook path past
machines whose
gears it kept
from combustion.
What could be
wrong, we thought,
with steel claiming
for itself a little
excess chill?

Later, the inclement
noses, the cranial
thrush & skelter.
But these are not
what finally fenced
the place, drove us
to the new town pool
with its goose
shit & conciliatory
slide. Instead
it was the month

one girl & then
another tied herself
to that fervid current,
sped beyond the call
of friends safely
inner-tubed, mothers
lunging up
from cotton

blankets, passed
a distant sandbar,
last scrap of
land in a nation-
state of water,
& dispersed.

SAVVY (ELEGY FOR GOOGLE GLASS)

My lenses have no further
plans than to correct myopia's

pulled-cotton frazzle of color
and line. I record nothing

I see—or rather only that which
impresses by whatever trick

of sentimentality and projection,
to be remixed later with errant

judgment, misrecalled odor, song
snippet, affiliated neural drek.

Memory: less faithful than film, itself
a specter absorbed into dot-matrix

vapor, like the spider who liquefies
what's solid in order to consume.

They say within the decade
we'll capture every moment,

cameras wedded to retina
or temple, digital lives cast

like second shadows,
dispassionate, searchable

surplus. We'll interrupt our arguments
to spectate our arguments,

shout at the selves caught
in the act of shouting at each other,

tip the mirror, live in infinite
reverb. We'll fret over storage,

live voluminous in airspace
suffocating with all the us

that's ever been.
Days will be made to extend

like clever cabinets, jangled
with shelves and accordion doors,

so we can slide out of the time
happening to us, into the time

in which we're happening,
our four eyes looking

forward, backward, askance,
but mainly outside-in.

COVER STORIES

It's true we didn't say, but also
no one thought to ask.
We'd carry my suitcase

to her bedroom at the top
of stairs her parents had built
with their own hands

& didn't wonder over. The walls
were slanted but the house stood
anyway. Her twin bed

crouched on lilac carpet. Later,
I was always walking two blocks
to a basement apartment,

the only warm place in the city.
I won't say if I was alone,
lying on my back, watching heat

bend the air along a ceiling pipe
wide as a culvert, which fed
every radiator in the building,

& was always on. Oh, sweet
sham: the love that dare not,
etc. Quiet now. The good

book sleeps on a red-spined
shelf. Color of sacrament,
of months passing. Even after

all this time, we remain terse,
our answers in recovery.
Grey clouds candle the night-

leaning sky. Summer ungenders.
We step out, our legs marveling
at every way we choose to go.

IT IS STILL TOO EARLY TO TALK ABOUT THE GECKOS' CAUSE OF DEATH

—on the return of the Russian Photon-M
research satellite, September 2014

For one, they were terribly
beautiful. Their gold skin

the color of celebrity eyelids
overlaid with plangent blue-green

and daubed red to match
the half-masks they wore

below their eyes—gestural
fine-art lizards, *ornate day geckos*

even science was obliged
to name them. Soft around the legs

and midsections, not a species
enamored of the appearance

of starvation, they preferred
to *lick soft, sweet fruit, pollen and*

nectar. We can't yet bring ourselves
to discuss how they perished,

only to say that they gleamed
marching into that capsule

and of those sent up—the mice,
the flies, the fungus—only

the geckos were equal
to the dark jewel of space.

IMPASSE

Yes   a fainting spell   a welt

  aching temples   a day home

from work   an ambulance

  a hospital stay   pharmaceuticals

  exercise   foods to increase, avoid

  surgeries, even if risky   medical

  trials   See   the possibilities

are endless, except   for how quickly

they ended   Friend   what peace

can be made   with death

  you have made it   but I'm still

angling for reprieve   Each September

  finds me   at this bargaining

table   with its single chair   sending

offers   into a quiet   that neither

echoes nor alters   the past

  asking no pardon   the present incomplete

VECTOR

Think of spirits
on the shelf of the liquor
store at 5th & Plum,

their flavor of stem
and petal, recipe unknown

to all but two living monks
these past 400 years.

Think of secrets
guarded that long.

Think of the plastic card
with its clumped digits
and mysterious chip

which reads plain
as speech to the simplest
machine.

Think of the far stars
announcing their births
after 10 billion years—

the time it takes light
to arrive.

Think of what is deliberately
excluded, how it sharpens
the edges of what's kept.

Think or don't,
sometimes you only
get sore reaching.

Start again.
In what direction?

Check the mail.
Someone's sent you
something beautiful.

Start there.

TAKE CARE, I LOVE YOU
—for S.D.

pick clothes up off the furniture.
cross the floor in a way your hips
appreciate. be greedy with breath.

turn the armchair to afternoon sun,
& when wind claws the house
corners, when the radio chants
numbers of the dead & missing,

when the computer calls all
to itself with its ingratiating
glow, try to catch the thread
the body sends up: hunger.

go out to the hen house,
select an egg. elsewhere,
our jobs thud & we mean
a lot with them. we come home
to quiet, a fearsome flower.

friend, I miss you. the weather
is grey here. the sky pinned
with clouds like the little white
draperies you make out of waxed
linen & kisses.

tell me. let's both break our hearts,
clear room for something more
mineral. let's fray these
suitable edges. let's shore.

at the end of your visit, I drove
you to the bus, waved
through the glass window.

you were never rushing.
you set down your bags.
counted change.

COPPER BASIN

That I still meet you
in memory. That your sudden,
ceaseless absence
doesn't   blizzard back
to cover what I've kept:

you in my tent one July,
knees drawn up as if legs

were excess—   that skimped
slip of nylon where I was afraid
          to sleep alone.

          Later your life brinked.
We blinked and it was over,
which is perhaps why I keep
          fearing you'll be plucked

from past along with present,
dropped-called
          from conversations
I didn't know I needed

to emboss in the mind's
electric filagree.

          So far
thank god or blind chance,
I think back and you

go on
      drifting beside me
      while heavenly bodies sift
thick as dust through the tent's mesh
      brim,

your breath unprecious,
      its fluttered path
      from the lungs' soft mineshaft
to the chill
of an altitude-tardy spring.

Crowned peaks close enough
      to count on, like the next day's
climb over rock
busy remembering
      its former life as fire—

the summit   where land rumpled
      away in all directions
and we crouched, keeping
our limbs low for balance, stood slowly,
      and didn't slip, not then.

"Dear Skull" was inspired by Paul Koudounaris's photographs of jeweled skeletons exhumed in Rome in the mid-1500s, as printed in *Heavenly Bodies: Cult Treasures and Spectacular Saints of the Catacombs*. Thank you to Jessica Walsh for sharing these photographs with me.

"It is Still Too Early to Talk about the Geckos' Cause of Death" takes its title from an official at the Russian Institute of Biomedical Problems, as quoted in *Russia Confirms the Death of Five Geckos on Space Sex Mission* (The Guardian, Sept 2014). The phrase "soft sweet fruit, pollen, and nectar," comes from *Three Endangered Yellow-Headed Day Geckos Born at Bristol Zoo* (ITV News, April 2015).

Thanks to Sam Cha for the title of "Effluvium."

The fourth stanza of "Introduction (At first I thought)" mirrors language from Mary Jo Bang's "The Beauties of Nature," especially the phrase "each gone beloved."

"The Springs" was inspired by photographs of tourists visiting Sol Duc Hot Springs in the early 1900s. Though now operated by the National Park Service, Sol Duc was a privately-owned luxury resort from 1912–1918. Sources suggest a member of the Quileute Nation first shared the location of the springs with a white settler as thanks for help healing from an injury. Subsequently, the settler made a homestead claim on the site and began charging an admission fee for its use.

"Equity" references Olympia, Washington's history as a sundown town, particularly for Black soldiers stationed at nearby Fort Lewis. Fort Lewis (now Joint Base Lewis-McCord) was officially segregated from 1918–1948. The base was established in 1917 when the U.S. Army forced members of the Nisqually Nation from their treatied territories, and later enlarged using a court process of "condemnation" which resulted in the theft of two-thirds of Nisqually land.

ACKNOWLEDGMENTS

Many thanks to the following publications in which these poems first appeared, occasionally in slightly different forms.

7x7.la: "Bodies"; "Vector"; "Equity"
Barrow Street: "Electromagnetic"
The Cortland Review: "Relativity"
The Georgia Review: "Dear Skull"
Gertrude Press: "Savvy (Elegy for Google Glass)"
The Gettysburg Review: "Erotica"
Juxtaprose: "Copper Basin"
The Massachusetts Review: "Effluvium"
NECK: "Chastened"
Nimrod: "Cover Stories"; "Introduction (Now there is no rush)"; "Span"
Poetry Northwest: "Houseboat"
RADAR: "Introduction (At least once)"; "Dusk; "Introduction (At first i thought)"; "Dénouement"
Rock & Sling: "Take Care", "I Love You"
Soil Dwellers (May Day Press, 2015): "Surface"
SpoKe: "Nonsomnolet"
Thalia: "It Is Still Too Early to Talk About the Geckos' Cause of Death"
Washington 129 (Sage Hill Press, 2017): "Memorial"

"En Sito" appears on Claudia Castro Luna's website *Washington Poetic Routes* (www.washingtonpoeticroutes.com).

"Dear Skull" was reprinted in *Best American Poetry,* 2017. Natasha Trethewey and David Lehmen, eds. Simon & Schuster, 2017.

"Surface" was first shown as a collaboration with the scientist Emilie Bess, the musician Mélanie Valera, and the the book artist Catherine Michaelis, at the exhibition *Dirt? Scientists, Book Artists, and Writers*

Reflect on Soil and Our Environment. University of Puget Sound, Tacoma, WA, August–December 2015.

Bodies and Vector were created as part *Every Cell Stand Still,* a collaboration with the fiber artist Sonja Dahl.

I am hugely grateful to the following people and organizations, along with many more friends, family, and fellow writers than I can name here, without whose support I could not have made this book:

Thanks to Michael Hoeye and Martha Banyas of the Far Lookout where many of these poems were first written.

Thanks to the staff and my incredible cohort at Civitella Ranieri. I am in awe of all of you, and can't imagine a better birthplace for this book.

Thanks to Mary Jo Bang for her close reading of several of these poems, to their extreme benefit.

Thanks to Natasha Trethewey, David Lehmen, the editors of *The Georgia Review* and *RADAR*, and the committee of the Tucson Book Festival Literary Awards for honors that placed some of these poems in hugely inspiring company.

Thanks to Lisa Ludden Perry and Alexandra Teague for crucial readings that found the heart of this collection and helped make it whole.

And to Allison, whose love is the best gift. Thank you for building me a room of my own, with all the bookshelves a girl could want.